MY HEART ON A SILVER PLATTER

WRITTEN BY:
JENNIFER MASSEY

My Heart on a Silver Platter

tellwell

Tellwell Talent
www.tellwell.ca

ISBN
978-0-2288-0793-3 (Hardcover)
978-0-2288-0792-6 (Paperback)

I'm scared to let people read this, I hid my feelings with a smile and covered my emotions with strength. Showing my vulnerability has always been something I chose not to show. My weaknesses were for me, and me only. These memories were supposed to fade with time, but they didn't, so here I am laying it out for the world to read, because I know I'm not the only one who's felt this heartache. The purpose of this book is for my readers to be inspired to change, to recognize their self-worth, and understand that our hearts are never broken forever, but for merely a small portion of our lives. It does get better. This is dedicated to the boys who broke my heart and the boys' hearts I've broken, the friends I've lost and the ones I've gained; and the daily turmoil I've dealt with thus far in my life. You made me who I am today, and this is my way of saying thank you.

UNCERTAINTY

Some of us choose the life we wanted,
without knowing if it's really what we want.

WINE

I drink to help me sleep,
I sleep to forget the pain.

LONELY

I sit, I sit in a room full of people.
I listen, I listen to the conversations.
Only to realize I was never apart of the circle,
merely a presence to fill the space.

JOKES ON ME

We grew together only to grow apart,
because you forgot the love I had for you
and replaced it with someone else's.

BELIEVE IN YOURSELF

Dreams are broken, by those who don't believe
in you. Don't let them break your spirit.
Dreams are created to help guide your future.
Never Let anyone tell you that you can't.

JOKES ON YOU

I think of you, how I loved you deeply
and how you threw my love
and replaced it for a foolish love.

A DARK PLACE

I sit in darkness because it comforts my
emotions and the feelings in my head. I see the light
and still I choose darkness.

LIGHT OF MY LIFE

Darkness has taken over me.
I forgot the feeling of light,
then I see your face and
I forget the darkness and see your light.

ONE IN A MILLION

You chose to not love me, but the thought of me.
You chose a love that you thought would replace mine
but you forgot one thing, my love is one of a kind.

EMPTINESS

I cry, because I know you are facing
the same pain as me.
Still you choose to stay where you are, without me
because you think it will stop you
from the pain you feel,
emptiness.

TOO MUCH

You feel empty because you
have given all of you,
only to realize that you are gone
because you have given too much.

DOMINO EFFECT

My heart chose you,
but you chose a heart
that never chose you.

THE BUTTERFLY EFFECT

I roll myself into a cocoon
only to wait for the day that I bloom.

CONCEALED BEAUTY

I look in the mirror only to find disgust
you look at me and find the beauty of a rose
which helps me to bloom.

AFTER LIFE

What I hold dear to me is the thought of you
being with me, not now, but one day in my arms
sitting in silence by the lake. With no thought or
feeling, but the sound of water hitting the rocks
beneath our feet with your presence near me.

SINKING

I'm drowning at the thought of our broken love
the love that once helped us float,
now together we drown in our very
own broken-hearted boats.

COFFEE FIRST

I step into the sun with my coffee
I take a sip and instantly, I feel at ease.

FORGIVENESS

Forgiving someone is hard
but forgiving yourself is even harder.

WHO AM I?

I stare into my eyes through the reflection
of the mirror, only to see someone who is not me.

HOME NOT SO SWEET HOME

I looked around in my home, feeling trapped
how could a place that's so sweet, feel so bitter?

FREEDOM

I wait for the day I fall into a deep sleep
for it is the only way I can be free.

REMINISCE

I picture us the way we used to be,
only now, it is in my dreams.

REGRET

I look back at the decisions I made,
the only regret I have is letting you go.

BROKEN DREAMS

What would life be like if we were together, we sat by the lake and envisioned a life, a life that could never be. We dreamt about our children, that would never exist, we pictured a home by the lake, that would never be built. We talked about our love, that we would never experience.

IS IT REAL?

I scroll through her pictures to see your face,
to see the smile that once was just as real with me
as it is with her.

SAVIOUR

She protects me from me.

ANXIETY ATTACK

I feel myself drowning as I cry
the shortness of breath and the pain in my chest.
I drown because I feel,
my tears drown me and slowly it kills me.

BURNING ALIVE

I felt alive in your arms, your touch made me glow.
Your smile filled my heart, You set my
heart on fire and I burn alive.

WASTED TIME

I stay awake glaring at the ceiling wondering and
thinking about the wasted days I spent with you,
a huge portion of my life now in your hands.

THE GIFTS

All these gifts you once gave me meant so much
they each have a story that shares our love
letting go of them, means letting go of you.

REBIRTH

Us humans are similar to a tree.
We grow old, we change, and we die
apart of us will always remain on earth.
We're just reborn from the roots.

ILLUSION

I thought I found love
only to find out it was a mirage
of a love that never existed.

I F**Ked up

I broke his heart thinking it would heal mine,
I found another thinking it would
mend my broken heart.
Only to realize I've always loved him,
only he has found another.

COLD

Love was what I had for you, but
you broke every part of me
that loved you, now I'm left with a cold
heart that feels nothing for you.

PSYCHO

Your love is toxic, yet I keep coming back
because I fear what you would do.

I CHOOSE ME

We are given one life
put yourself first.

TAKER

He sucked the happiness out of me and still I stay
wondering and looking into the
mirror trying to find my smile.

DEAD INSIDE AND OUT

Every bit of happiness was ripped out
of my soul, that I could feel no more.

NO LONGER MATERIALISTIC

I tried to find happiness in things, only to realize I had to find happiness within.

DRIED OUT

I cried so many tears that I could no longer cry. Like
the sun drying out the water on earth. I wanted
to feel something, feel my wet tears run down
my face. My tears represented my love for you
I knew that if it were to stop, it meant my heart
was slowly unloving you. Forcing me to let go.

LESSONS

I look back at the decisions I've made
I regret nothing.

QUIET THOUGHTS

Even on the most silent of nights
I think of you. The memory of you haunts me everyday.
I lay my head to rest, and close my eyes in hopes that
I no longer remember you. But it's the quiet
nights that I find torture me the most.

COLD SHOULDER

I waited for you to say I love you, instead
you turned your back and forgot about me.
You never tried to find me or ask how I was doing.
I no longer existed, you erased me
out of your life forever.

ALCOHOLIC

He drank to clear his mind, I thought I was his cure.
That my love would change him, but it was the alcohol
that he thought would cure him,
only it destroyed him.

LUSTFUL THOUGHTS

I pictured his lips on mine,
his body pressing against me,
His hands all over my body.
I bit my lips with just the thought of his face
for so long I desired him.
After the kiss we shared, we couldn't resist
I knew then he desired me too.
We had to feel each other just once
the passion was always there
and still it continues.

STAR-CROSSED LOVERS

I gazed at the sky hoping you were watching too
thinking of me the way I was thinking of you.

HELPLESS

I felt nothing as if I were stuck
in a dark depressing hole.
I was trapped inside my own body, as if
someone had taken over me. I'm still finding
a way to escape. Waiting for the old happier
me to break through this heartache,
I want to feel the happiness I once felt.
I want to be the old me.

BLANK STARE

I longed for an answer, one that I thought I could get.
I wanted to feel his love, the love he once had for me
I hoped I would find it looking into him.
I remember those loving eyes, I used to feel the
passion when he would stare at me, this time I looked
into his eyes searching for it and I saw nothing.

LIAR

Too many times they hurt you
too many times they lied.
Too many times they made promises
too many just turned into more lies.

READY, SET, GO...

You spent years loving him
without him ever knowing, It's
finally time to tell him.

FAKE FRIENDS

Our friendship was more important to
me than anything, you destroyed it
by stabbing me in the back.

ON MY MIND

When I close my eyes, I see you.

I'M ENOUGH

I lay in my bed with my eyes filled with
tears, wondering how my love was never
enough for you.

NO LONGER A VIRGIN

He forced me to lay with him
I was still, my young mind not knowing what to do.
I didn't want this to happen, but
I was broken and weak
I could no longer feel.
I let him in me, and I regret it everyday.

KEEP WATCHING

Don't ever let anyone tell you, *you can't*, because
the same people who said that to me
are now watching me do it.

POINT PROVEN

He told me I couldn't do anything without him
as if I was dependant on him, I wasn't.
I felt a sense of determination
I was angry with how little he thought of me.
I never wanted to feel that way again
so, I left him and showed him I could.
I will never let a man think of me
as being small or weak
I depend on me, and me only.

AT PEACE

How I wish to be a bird spreading my wings
and soaring freely into the sunset.

THE POWER OF VOICE

Use your voice as strength,
speak what's on your mind, and
believe what you say.
Your voice has power.

IT'S TIME

Say *"I love you"* before it's too late
you'll regret it forever, trust me.

CLOUD 9

He put his hands on me, he spread my legs
and magnetized my soul.

SUPERGLUE

He shattered the depth of my soul and spirit
like a cracked mirror that was thrown
on the floor. My fingers bleed while
I try to match the pieces, feeling every bit of
pain trying to put myself back together.

SCARS

The ones who broke my heart left a scar
each with a story, each with a lesson.

HIDDEN AWAY

I smile to hide the pain, I laugh to avoid the cry.
I wear a mask, so no one can see the real me.

ANGRY

You waited for me to turn my back,
so you could stab a knife through it.
Kind of like a syringe filled with poison, instead you
filled my soul with hatred and anger,
using that knife. Never wanting
to trust or love anyone,
ever.

VISION

I looked into your eyes and saw the sunrise.

YOUR LOSS

Don't ever worry about people who left you behind
chances are every time you look
back they will be staring.

INSOMNIA

I sit in the dark room listening to my thoughts
swirling around in my head, loosing sleep and
getting dizzy, wanting it to stop.
How can I erase these thoughts?
-It never goes away.

SAFE ZONE

I held his hand and felt a sense of security
I knew then he would protect me.

MY HEART SINGS YOUR NAME

I put his hand to my chest, "*listen to it beat*"
I said, this is a song I wrote for you.

THE RAVINE

We walked the path we always walked
It was our route to school.
The trees moved in the wind
and the birds chirped early in the morning. With the
sun shining down on us. We stopped at the bridge
and stood there for a moment.
We stared at one another in
silence holding each other,
from that moment I knew I loved
you and that you did too.

OUR MEETING SPOT

I walked towards him
The sky was black as night.
The street lights were turned on
with the stars shinning down on us,
he stood under the gazebo waiting, his back turned.
It had been years since I'd seen
his face,
as he turned around to look at me
I felt my stomach turn, nervously I continued to walk.
The moon lit up his face, and I felt the love I first felt
when we were young and in love.

NEVER LET GO

I hugged him every time I left
not knowing that it would
one day be the last time I held him.

PRETEND

Social media has become our world
We are the set designers, for a desired life
that is staged. Fake images posted on our pages
to show the world something we are not.

EVERYTHING HAPPENS FOR A REASON

After many months I hadn't seen
you, we decided to meet.
I was nervous, afraid I'd fall in love
again. Once we finally met
I realized why we would have never worked.

OVER THE YEARS

I always thought of him, I blamed
myself for loosing you.
I wanted you back, by then you
had already forgotten me.
-Nothing left to do but move on.

YOUR PRESENCE

I felt my stomach turn, seeing
him always felt like an adrenaline rush.
I saw him from a distance, and
felt my heart beat faster.

WISER

As I grow older I realize that the mistakes
I made helped me to become who I am.

AWKWARD

I was so excited to talk to him
I was looking forward to seeing him all day,
we met and had nothing to talk about.
We sat in silence, pushing ourselves to talk
repeating the same things
and mumbling our words.
Our faces flushing, as red as an apple
It felt like a first date
only this time it would be our last.

ICE BOX

My heart turned cold and black
I could feel my heart beat slowly beginning to
Stop. Love no longer existed inside of me.
I wrapped my heart and placed
It into a box, freezing it,
preventing anyone from getting in.
I decided I was never going to love
I was going to protect it,
Hide it away.
I would never let anyone
break it ever again.

WARM HUG

He wrapped his arms around me
I wished he'd never let go.

INDEPENDENT

Just remember, it's only you that
can change your life around
never depend on anyone changing it, but yourself.

DRUNKEN THOUGHTS

As I drink this glass of rum
I stare at the wall with a blank glare.
I feel myself dosing off
and I begin to wonder about my life,
I start to think about the past and
how I could have changed it.
I live through these thoughts over and over
not knowing if these changes would have
ever benefited me or made me happier.
My anger begins to emerge
and I blame myself for my choices.
I drink more hoping
It will knock me out, the only thing to
save me now is drinking till
I fall asleep.

DEEPER MEANING

How are we supposed to live
in a world that compares their life to others?
We've forgotten about us.

ZERO COMMUNICATION

We sit across from each other in silence.
We're close to one another, yet we feel so distant.
Our bodies slouching over, staring closely
at the screens of our phones, as
the white light shines brightly into our eyes.
We forget each other exist,
having conversations through text with people
who are not physically there
but forgetting about the ones who are.
How sad have our relationships become?

ROBOT'S

Our screens on our phone
have control over our minds.
We no longer long for human interaction,
but internet access.

DISAPPEARING

Slowly my memory of you fades
I no longer see your face in my dreams.
I am now lost in them
walking down a foggy path
where I cannot see.
Secretly searching for you, knowing I shouldn't.
Hoping you appear from the fog
now all I see is a shadow of you
slowly fading away. I want to see your face
but I know it's time,
it's time to let go.

NO MORE

One day you'll think of me everyday
the way I did, and I will have already forgotten you.

TATTOO

I carved your name into my heart
knowing it would never be erased.

PERFECT

I love every part of you
even the parts that drive me crazy.

SET MY HEART ON FIRE

I light my candle as if it were your heart
hoping it will never burn out.

#1

If I could go back in time
I would have always chosen you.

CONSTANTLY THERE

I thought of you daily, as I opened
my eyes to start the day
and as I closed them. Closing my
eyes was the best part
because I knew that I would see you.

DESPERATE

You said you weren't ready to be in a relationship
yet it only took you a short while to find another,
another to feed lies to.

THE ONLY ONE

Soon you will realize that my love was
genuine, rare, and true. By then I will
have forgotten all about you, and I will have
finally stopped loving you.

SET MY SOUL ON FIRE

His touch lit a fire in me
we connected, and I knew
then that you had to be mine.

IT'S EASY

Happiness is a choice
that seems to be the hardest to choose.

FAST FORWARD

I pictured our life in the future, it was perfect.

INNISFIL

I remember us sitting by the beach
feet in the water, and the sun in our face
how I wish to get back that time where we were one.

ONE BY ONE

Slowly I put my heart back together
like puzzle pieces scattered on the floor.

EVERY PART OF ME

I looked at you, not just with my heart
but with my soul.

ERASING YOU

Writing my feelings helps me to forget you.

JUNE

Summer was the season
I fell in love with you.

YOU LOST HER

I realize now you never
loved me the way I loved you.

HE'S OUT THERE

Life is short don't live it loving someone
who doesn't love you back.

TRYING TO GET OVER YOU

It kills me to see you happy
while I sit here miserable thinking of you.

WITH TIME

You don't need a man to mend your heart
you can do that all on your own, be strong.

I AM

Look yourself in the mirror
and say you're beautiful.

KARMA

You finally felt what I felt
after all these years,
only after you saw that
I was happy once again.

REMEMBER ME

Don't sit there and wait for him to love you
help him to remember why he once loved you.

MANIPULATOR

When you finally decide to walk away
that's when he'll choose you, don't give in.

LOOSE CHAINS

Let go of your past mistakes,
past lovers, just let it all go.

OUT OF TIME

I took too long to say I love you.

BEST DECISION

I am now learning to accept
where I am in life and move on.

YOU'RE THE PROBLEM

You hold me back with your lies and promises
I always give in, not this time.

STITCHING IT ALL TOGETHER

I found myself, sewing my own heart together.
The needle slowly piercing in and out of my heart
covering my open wounds, healing the ache one stitch
at a time. At that moment I realized that
I had become my own healer.

CRUSH

I was young, I thought I knew what
love was, boy was I crazy.

ROTTEN

I lost my virginity to a monster an experience
that was supposed to be sweet and romantic,
only it turned into a rotten memory.

THE GARDENER

Keep your garden safe
only share it with the person
that helps you water and grow it.

WEAK & VULNERABLE

I was taken advantage of
I helplessly begged him to stop,
still he used his strength to control me
and I stayed silent.

COMPARING THE TWO

For all the time he was cruel to me I thought of you and how I made the biggest mistake letting you go.

THE ONE

Karma hit me when
I chose him over you.

I'M SORRY

I bet you he regrets all
the pain he caused you.

COMPARISON

Stop comparing your life to others
your life is just as beautiful as theirs.

TURN AWAY

It's okay to let go of toxic people in your life, your happiness comes first.

MAMA KNOWS BEST

Growing up, my mom always said "*your friends will one day betray you,*" mama knows best.

09.22.17

I dreamt of the day
I would marry you
that dream came true.

SIDE BY SIDE

You were there through
my darkest times
and through my brightest.

I GOT YOUR BACK

Your true character shows
when someone
talks badly about your friend.

WHAT IS SUCCESS?

You are only successful
if you are happy with your life,
that is true success.

MIND OVER EVERYTHING

You learn to love yourself
when you change your mindset.

TRAVEL

I found peace by
finding beauty in this world.

PERFECT

You are God's perfect creation.

ON A MISSION

Your life has a purpose on this earth, search for it.

HOPELESS PLACE

We thought our love would survive
but the universe forbids it.

WAITING TO REINCARNATE

We belong together not in this life, but the next.

LOVE STRUCK

I kissed his lips and instantly
I regretted it because I never wanted it to stop.

ANOTHER SIDE

Don't worry about
what people post
on social media,
pictures don't always
say a thousand words.

MODERN LOVE

Our love isn't real unless
it's posted on Instagram.

BETRAYAL

Be careful who you share
your weaknesses with,
those same people use that
as their weapon against you.

TRUE FRIENDSHIP

She shared your secrets with me,
I stayed quiet because I didn't want to see you hurt.

IN MY BUBBLE

I decided to hide away
my fear and anxiety,
I created a shield hoping
no one will get through.

NEVER GETTING IT BACK

Wasted time is what hurts the most.

IGNORED

I blame myself, for having my heart broken
I keep falling in love with a man
who doesn't even notice me.

TOOK YOU LONG ENOUGH

I hope one day you approach me and say *"I have always loved you."*

PEDESTAL

Don't let him walk all over you
respect yourself enough to say
you deserve better.

ON MY FEET

Never give them the chance to see you fall
only let them see you rise.

STAND TALL

Never show your vulnerability
show them your strength.

QUENCHED

I realize the more he ignored me
the more I craved him.

BLINDED

The sad thing is you only
noticed me when I left.

PATIENCE IS KEY

Before you know it
all the things you hoped would happen
will eventually happen, be patient.

POSITIVE VIBES

Surround yourself with people that support you
not the ones who degrade you.

EMPOWERING FRIENDS

Surround yourself with people that
build you up, not tear you down.

BE YOU

Focus on finding someone
who loves you for you,
don't change who you are
to get their attention.

ACTIONS SPEAK THE LOUDEST

It's the simple actions
that mean the most.

THEY'RE OUT THERE

Just because one person hurt you
doesn't mean everyone else will,
pick and choose who you let in wisely.

ONE OF A KIND

She's a rare woman, one that you cannot have,
one that you can only admire from afar
she's the woman that always crosses your mind.

SIMPLY DONE

I've grown tired of dealing with the same issues
I'm about to give up on you.

LADDER

Don't worry about the process
just think about the progress,
you're almost there.

FEMINIST

Remind him that you can be strong even without him.

6th SENSE

A woman's intuition was created
so she can protect herself.

HESITANT

I got closer and closer to the edge
'til finally you pushed me off.

FROZEN

I can feel my body going numb
my heart beating fast, and
my lips sealing closed.
Every time I see you
I get butterflies.

FORGOTTEN

The attention you don't give to her
will be found from another
cherish her, don't take her for granted.

DEAR...

He wrote me letters everyday
sharing his love for me.
I held them close to my heart
I hope you know how important you were to me,
I'm sorry I didn't love you the same way.

SHIT TALKERS

It doesn't matter
they're going to talk
about you
so let them talk.

ON A SEARCH

I'm still trying to figure out what love is.

IS SHE WORTH IT?

She's not an easy one to get
she's trapped within the walls she's built,
you have to break down those walls to get to her.

SOMETHING I'M NOT

I started to change, I wanted to impress you
make you fall in love with me, make you want me,
I realized how pathetic I had become.

WHEREVER YOU ARE

I would move mountains and
cross oceans just to see you.

MISSED CALLS

I called you every summer hoping
you'd pick up the phone
I wanted to tell you I loved you, but
my tongue always held back
as if the universe knew it wasn't meant for you.

WHY NOW?

You called me that day
I waited for years for that call.
My heart stopped as I looked at the phone
"why did you have to call me so late?"
I thought to myself
I'd already given myself to someone else.

THE LAST PIECE

I finally got up and left, while I was gone
you didn't know what to do.
You called for me to come back,
you felt alone, and weak
I hope now you understand that I'm the
puzzle piece that completes your life.

PROUD

I finally embraced the
beauty of my imperfections.

LONDON

We share our love across oceans
craving to touch and hold one
another through the night,
our hearts connected through phones
but separated by water.

FALSE TEACHINGS

Our religion forbids us to be with one another
yet our religions teach us to love.

ME BEFORE YOU

I would give up my life
just to share it with you.

HIS PUPPET

He controlled me like a puppet doll, and I allowed it.
what an idiot I was, for I thinking this was love.

YOUR OWN PERCEPTION

I wouldn't ever call myself a writer
just a girl who has a story to share
but allowing you to perceive my words in your way.

NOW YOU SEE ME, NOW YOU DON'T

Girls have a habit of letting go of friendships
because of their relationships
what a sad and stupid way to live.

LIGHTS, CAMERA, ACTION

It doesn't matter if your doing well or bad in your life.
Just remember there's an audience
and the show must go on,
Keep your head up.

NOT THE SAME

The sad part is I thought
you loved me
the way I loved you.

CHECK YOUR POCKET

If there was one thing I would say to the old me
I would say never depend on anyone but yourself,
you are the key to your own happiness.

SOCIETIES EXPECTATIONS

Our minds have been filled with false advertisements
about how a woman should look. We feel as
though we need to change who we are. We look
at ourselves in disgust, finding ways to cover our
imperfections with make-up and injections.
We're forced to compete with one another,
as we explore Instagram, we begin to
wonder if we're good enough.
If we're even desirable or loveable.
We have made our lives into a competition,
us woman are making ourselves sick.

HANDS OFF

You think you can touch me the way you want
as if you own me, I belong to no one but myself.

FADED AWAY

I saw you as a friend, I thought of
the days we were young
and the memories we shared. I thought
they were just as important
to you as they were to me, I was wrong.

FORGOT HOW TO LOVE

Love has become a word that we
throw around like word vomit,
we've forgotten the sacredness of
this powerful word, love.

VINTAGE

You moved away, you were able to forget our love
I'm stuck in the same neighbourhood
where we walked, talked, and shared
memories. How could I have forgotten so
easily when I was surrounded by you?

SOLO

Can't take it anymore
I'm going to do this on my own
I've learnt to do everything
Independently, I'm no longer
letting you hold me back.

RUMOUR HAS IT

You lied, you spread rumours about me.
You created a false image of me,
and let everyone think it was true.

POWER OF MUSIC

Music was the cure for my soul
as I listened to the words of the songs
I felt my heart slowly beating again.

LOOK WHO'S LAUGHING NOW

Remember the time I shared my
dreams, and you laughed?
It's funny now that I've accomplished
those same dreams
you no longer have anything to laugh about.

BITTER

All I can say now is, fuck you!

GOODBYE FOREVER

He looked so peaceful when he
slept, I looked at him lovingly
I whispered *"I love you,"* hoping he'd hear me.
I gently kissed his forehead, picked up my
things and silently left his life forever.

CONTROLLED

I felt horrible for what I did, it was a sinful act.
My mind was saying no, but my body was saying yes.

FORGET IT EVER HAPPENED

I knew he loved me, but he knew that
he was too late to have me.
So much had happened over the years between us
that he thought it could never work,
I thought differently.

HIGH SCHOOL SWEETHEARTS

What a beautiful love story we would
have had if we stayed together. Middle
school lovers, to high school lovers
to one day being husband and wife.
Our paths chose differently.

NO BAD DAYS

Our minds have complete control over everything
that happens in our lives.
If we think and feel positive, there will
always be positive outcomes.
Control your mind and great things
will come, I promise.

MONEY COMES, MONEY GOES

We live in a selfish generation , we thirst for money.
It has become the evil of this world.
The main priority of our lives,
not to say money is not important
but we have forgotten how to live.

LOYALTY

There is no better quality in friendship than loyalty
stick to those people, they'll be
your ride or die friends.

TWO FACED

You wear your mask with me
then take it off as soon as you leave,
I don't know who you are,
you become someone else.

WINDOWS TO THE SOUL

Look into their eyes, it will tell you everything
you want to know.

SELFLESS

I made the mistake of loving you first before me.

BUILD

Work to build and create your own happiness,
never let anyone think they did it for you.

SHATTERED INNOCENCE

I was a child; my mind was innocent.
I thought we were playing a game, only
To you it was something more, now
that I'm older I know what you did.
It wasn't a game after all
you should be ashamed.

I LEARNED TO BE WITHOUT YOU

We did everything together,
shared the same sadness,
happiness, and excitement. We were inseparable
The whole world knew it,
Our friendship was rare and beautiful.
You destroyed it by choosing to
put those memories aside
and pushing me to the edge.

ME

I remember a time where I thought
I'd never be able to
heal from our breakup,
I didn't know how to love
anything else except you,
then I started noticing me
and I had a new person to love.

CLEARING

I was hurt with what you did
I hope you know, time has passed
and I have learned to forgive you,
but most importantly I learned to
forget you.

CHANGE

Change has the power to do incredible things
the fear of not knowing what may
happen next in your life.
That's the thrill of it all,
you won't know until you decide
that you want it to happen.

MOVING FORWARD

I learned to be strong with the mistakes I made,
for these same mistakes helped me take better steps
towards life.

BELONGING TO NOTHING

We feel the need to belong,
to belong to someone.
It's human nature I guess
but we've made the mistake of thinking
we should settle for less,
less than what we deserve. We are given
one life to live, and if that means letting go
of toxic relationships, then it's time to free
yourself and indulge in a new beginning,
It's better to be alone than to feel trapped.

PLAIN AND SIMPLE

I've seen too many women stick around
with asshole men and think that it is
normal to be treated in such a way.
Why have we given men the right
to treat us like that?
It's simple, because you allowed it.

BOSS

Look yourself in the mirror everyday,
and say you can do it
trust me darling, you can.

QUEEN

Don't ever put a man on a pedestal,
they learn to forget that it's you that belongs there.

WHO COULD IT BE?

Even after reading this book
you'll go about your day
oblivious to the fact that these
Words were meant for you.

LOST EYES

Her eyes once shined when you stared into her.
There was a glow upon her face, where did it go?
That shine, and that glow fell out of her eyes
from the tears she cried trying to love you.

STUCK

It was like my feet were glued to the floor.
I watched you walk away, my heart was telling me
to chase after you, but my body forced me not to.

FALSE DISPLAY

Our love is like a play
We want to put on a good show for the audience.
We display what love should look like,
giving the world a false idea of love.
We're stuck in this play, like a contract
With no escape.
Once the curtains close, the acting stops
that's when we both feel free.

STILL LOOKING

I've lost me trying to find you.

WORKING MACHINE

Every month we bleed
uncomfortable and in pain.
Yet we go about our day
trying to fight the world.
Working long hours, only to come home
to more work.
Caring for our home and our families
while still bleeding.
We're uncomfortable, we're in pain
but even bleeding from our own bodies
Never stops us from working.

WALKING CORPSE

I was alive, but I felt dead inside.
You'd never know it, looking at me
smiling at work,
smiling at home,
smiling in front of family and friends
adding a laugh here and there.
You'd think I was the happiest person alive
when really, I was dying inside. Living a lie.
You'd never know that I was breaking
you were looking at me, but were you looking
Inside me?

FREE

As I wrote these words, I felt as though
I wrote them with my own blood.
I see the words written in bright red
as if I spilled my pain into these pages
the pain I bottled into my heart, is now free.

EXPRESS

Our feelings are what make us unique, each with a story to tell. We tend to hide our feelings into the depths of our soul and sometimes prevent ourselves from showing it, why? These emotions that we experience daily make us grow, change, and adapt to our lives. Each with a lesson and a test. Don't ever take your feelings as a sign of weakness but as a sign of strength. Heartbreaks are the best of them all, because we learn to mend them ourselves, and that my friends is the bravest thing you could ever do.

CPSIA information can be obtained
at www.ICGtesting.com
Printed in the USA
LVHW050110180519
618323LV00001B/122/P

9 780228 807926